The Best You

Win or Lose

Kristy Stark, M.A.Ed.

Publishing Credits

Rachelle Cracchiolo, M.S.Ed., *Publisher*
Conni Medina, M.A.Ed., *Managing Editor*
Nika Fabienke, Ed.D., *Series Developer*
June Kikuchi, *Content Director*
John Leach, *Assistant Editor*
Kevin Pham, *Graphic Designer*

Image Credits: All images from iStock and/or Shutterstock.

Library of Congress Cataloging-in-Publication Data

Names: Stark, Kristy, author.
Title: The best you : win or lose / Kristy Stark, M.A.Ed.
Description: Huntington Beach, CA : Teacher Created Materials, [2018] | Audience: K to grade 3.
Identifiers: LCCN 2017029999 (print) | LCCN 2017055152 (ebook) | ISBN 9781425853259 (eBook) | ISBN 9781425849511 (pbk.)
Subjects: LCSH: Competition (Psychology)--Juvenile literature.
Classification: LCC BF637.C47 (ebook) | LCC BF637.C47 S73 2018 (print) | DDC 155.42/49--dc23
LC record available at https://lccn.loc.gov/2017029999

Teacher Created Materials
5301 Oceanus Drive
Huntington Beach, CA 92649-1030
http://www.tcmpub.com

ISBN 978-1-4258-4951-1

Printed by: 590835
Printed in: Taiwan

Two teams play.

One team wins.

One team loses.

Have fun.

Cheer for everyone.

Do your best.

Try again if you lose.

Be kind when you win.

Be kind when you lose.

Everyone played a great game!